ADRENALINE RUSH

WINDSURFING & KITE SURFING

ANNE-MARIE LAVAL

A⁺

Smart Apple Media

Published by Smart Apple Media,
an imprint of Black Rabbit Books
P.O. Box 3263, Mankato, Minnesota 56002
www.blackrabbitbooks.com

Printed in the United States of America at
Corporate Graphics, North Mankato, Minnesota.

Published by arrangement with the
Watts Publishing Group LTD, London.

Library of Congress Cataloging-in-Publication Data

Laval, Anne-Marie.
Windsurfing and kite surfing / Anne-Marie Laval.
p. cm.—(Adrenaline rush)
Includes bibliographical references and index.
Summary: "Explains the origins, techniques, and
equipment used in windsurfing and kite surfing.
Also details how the sports differ and who the
top athletes are in each sport. Features famous
and elite destinations and emphasizes the need
for proper training, equipment, and safety while
participating"—Provided by publisher.
ISBN 978-1-59920-683-7 (library binding :
alk. paper)
1. Windsurfing—Juvenile literature. 2. Kite
surfing—Juvenile literature. I. Title.
GV811.63.W56L38 2013
797.3'3--dc23
                                    2011053498

Produced by Tall Tree Ltd

PO1433
2-2012

9 8 7 6 5 4 3 2 1

Picture credits:
Cover, front: Dmitry Tsvetkov/Dreamstime.com
Cover, back: Rjmiguel/Dreamstime.com
1 Max Earey/Shutterstock, 4 Manolis Tsantakis/
Dreamstime.com, 5 Pierre-yves Babelon/
Dreamstime.com, 6 Patrick Ward/Corbis,
7t Hoch Zwei, 7b ohrim/Shutterstock,
8 Federico Donatini/Dreamstime.com,
9 Alexander Kolomietz/Dreamstime.com,
10 Dmitry Tsvetkov/Dreamstime.com,
11 sashagala/Shutterstock, 12-13 Tiziano Casalta/
Dreamstime.com, 13t Tiziano Casalta/
Dreamstime.com, 13b Juan Medina/Reuters/
Corbis, 14 Paul Topp/Dreamstime.com,
15 Max Earey/ Shutterstock, 16 Ana del Castillo/
Shutterstock, 17 ohrim/ Shutterstock, 18 Ben
Welsh/Corbis, 19c Djo Vander Linden/Dreamstime.
com, 19b Anna Chow/GNU, 20–21 Olga Makina/
Dreamstime.com, 21 Adrien Freville, 22-23
Nomadz/GNU, 23t Gamma-Rapho/Getty Images,
23b Odyssée du Vent, 24-25 ADI WEDA/epa/
Corbis, 25 Atm2003/Dreamstime.com,
26–27 Robert Hardholt/Shutterstock.com,
27 Ben Welsh/Corbis, 28 Pliene/Dreamstime.com,
29 Max Earey/Shutterstock.com

Words in **bold** are in the glossary on page 30.

CONTENTS

Imagine skimming along the surface of the sea. The board under your feet skips across the **chop**, and suddenly you launch into the air for a massive jump. That is kite surfing or windsurfing: two different ways to get the same kind of thrill.

Windsurfing

Windsurfers use a surfboard-like board and a sail. The equipment is bulkier than kiting gear, but once the board and sail are rigged up, the thrill of skimming across the tops of the waves is mind-blowing. Windsurfing can also be done in very light winds—winds where kites may not work.

A windsurfer uses a wave to flip himself into the air. Controlling the landing is the tricky part, though!

Kite Surfing

Kite surfers use large kites to drag their small boards across the sea, big lakes, or even rivers. One of the advantages of kite surfing is that your equipment can be carried easily in a backpack, with your board under your arm. You can catch the bus to the beach, then go kiting!

A kite surfer skims along a lagoon in northern Madagascar.

Top Two DVDs
- AC Extreme Kitesurfing—*some of the world's best kite surfers, including Mark Doyle and Aaron Hadlow, show off in fantastic locations around the world.*
- KA1111—*the first movie ever made by wave-sailing genius Jason Polakow, this is now an all-time classic.*

A windsurfer stands by his board. By the 1990s, boards had become much lighter and more fun to use.

Windsurfing and kite surfing are both quite new sports. Windsurfing took time to become popular, but kite surfing took off very quickly after it appeared in the late 1990s.

Born in California, Robbie Naish moved to Hawaii when he was a small boy. He started windsurfing at 11, and won his first world title at 13 years old. He went on to win 10 more windsurfing world championships. In the 1990s, Naish got into the new sport of kite surfing and won three more world titles.

The Windsurfing Craze

Windsurfing first became popular in the 1970s. Before then, if you wanted to go sailing you needed a boat. Windsurfing gear was far cheaper and much easier to move around than boats. Even so, the original boards were heavy and hard to ride. The designs quickly improved, and in the 1980s, windsurfing really took off. Suddenly, just about every beach in the world was decorated with brightly colored sails.

Kite Surfing Kicks Off

Kite surfing as we know it today developed in the 1990s, but kiting first became popular in the 2000s. Today, it is one of the fastest-growing ocean board sports. Many surfers are into kite surfing, because when it's too windy to go surfing, the conditions are often ideal for kiting instead.

This kite surfer is riding a double-ended board, which is popular for tricks on flat water.

Windsurfing and kiting have split into lots of different disciplines. Which discipline people follow depends on whether they are sailing on the ocean or fresh water.

These windsurfers are racing on a lake in Italy. In the background you can see one of the course-marker buoys and a boat with the race officials in it.

Fresh Water

Inland kiting and windsurfing mainly happen on big lakes and reservoirs because they have enough room for the riders to get going. Freshwater sailing tends to focus on **blasting** or **free riding**. The waves are rarely big enough for more radical wave-sailing tricks. However, a few rivers, such as the Columbia River in Oregon, offer advanced surfers the chance to show off their skills.

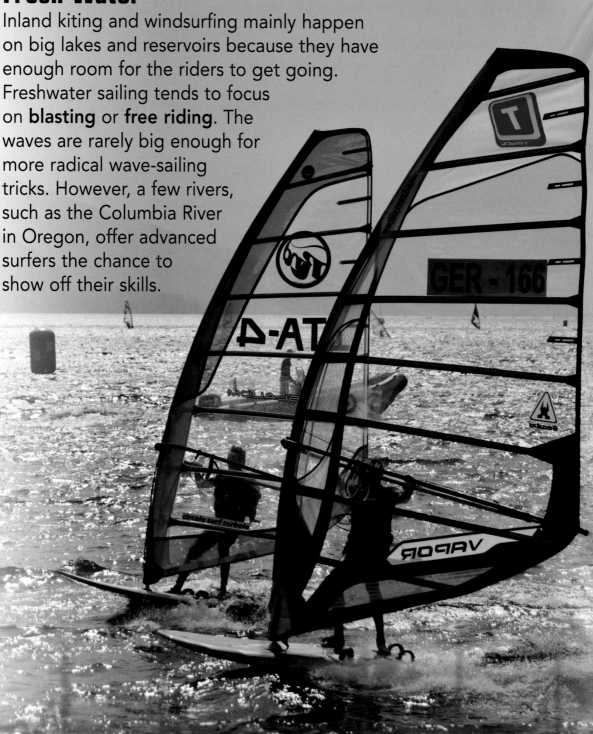

Kite surfers are attached to their kite with a harness. The harness spreads the force from the kite across the body, taking the strain away from the arms.

Don't Try This at Home
In the movie Die Another Day, secret agent James Bond kite surfs a car hood along a huge wave, using a parachute. This is a CGI stunt—it would be impossible in real life!

Ocean Sailing

For both windsurfing and kite surfing, ocean sailing is divided into two key styles of riding: flat water and wave.

• On flat water, both kiters and windsurfers tend to focus on whizzing in and out from the beach at high speed, throwing in a spectacular jump or turn every once in a while. This is often called blasting or free riding.

• On waves, the emphasis is on either using the waves as launch ramps for big jumps on the way out from the beach or riding the waves like a super-powered surfer on the way back in.

The biggest difference between a windsurf board and a kite board is size. The smallest windsurf board is far bigger than the largest kite board. The sails and kites also look completely different.

Windsurfing Equipment

There are boards and sails for different conditions. The two extremes are wave sailing and light-wind windsurfing:

• Wave sailing uses a small board, and a sail with a high-cut bottom edge (as shown here) so that it does not catch in the surf.

• Light-wind equipment includes a wide board and large sail with a low-cut bottom edge.

Masts are usually made of carbon fiber and designed to bend as the sail tightens. Sails are made of lightweight, waterproof fabric.

Battens are strips of plastic inside sleeves that run across the sail. They hold the sail in a curved shape to catch the wind.

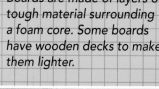

Boards are made of layers of tough material surrounding a foam core. Some boards have wooden decks to make them lighter.

Turned upside down, a kite can be carried easily by one person. If it was right side up, it could lift you into the air.

The kite gets its shape from tubes pumped full of air, similar to a tire. They have to be tough and flexible enough to survive multiple crashes.

Kite Surfing Equipment

In kite surfing, the main choice of boards is between one with footstraps, which is great for tricks and jumps, and one without. People select a kite depending on how windy it is. In lighter winds, a bigger kite is needed to get you moving. There are two main types of kites:

• Leading Edge Inflatables (LEIs), which have a straighter shape.

• Bow kites, which have a curved shape. Bow kites can be used in a wider range of wind speeds than LEIs.

Top How-To DVDs
• **Progression Kiteboarding**—*this series of kite surfing DVDs is an excellent aid to learning, for everyone from complete beginners to experts.*
• **Beginner to Winner**—*renowned windsurfing coach Jem Hall takes the viewer from basic techniques to advanced skills.*

ON THE SCREEN

FREESTYLE FUN

After a while, blasting in and out from the beach on your kite board just isn't enough. Even a long **downwinder** to another beach won't satisfy you. It's time to start throwing in some **freestyle** tricks—the techniques that make shore-bound spectators gasp in admiration.

Aerial Action

Kite surfers get added **hang time** from the lifting action of the kite. Because the kite holds them up in the air, they seem to go into slow motion almost as soon as they take off. The most skilled riders use this hang time to perform amazing tricks.

Complicated freestyle spins and twists like these always draw "Oohs" and "Ahhs" from people watching on the beach.

When something goes wrong, kite boarders let go of the bar they use to control the kite. This causes the kite to hover harmlessly in the air above them.

Freestyle Tricks

These are some of the most popular types of freestyle tricks:

• Grabs: holding the board with one hand

• Spins: spinning round and round in the air

• Board-offs: taking one or both feet off the board

• Inverts: any trick done upside down

• Kite loops: looping the kite around 360 degrees while doing a spin

Aaron Hadlow is arguably the best freestyle kite surfer ever. He won his first world championship at just 15 years old, and went on to win four more titles in a row. Since 2010, he has been working to further develop kites and boards.

One of the most exciting forms of windsurfing is wave sailing. At surf spots around the world, from Hawaii to Australia to the Canary Islands, you see excited windsurfers **rigging up** on days when the wind is blowing and the surf is up.

In wave sailing, a vertical takeoff like this can only mean one thing: this windsurfer is trying to do a loop.

Wave Sailing Part 1: Getting Out

For regular surfers, getting out to where the waves are breaking usually involves a long, hard paddle. For windsurfers, however, getting out is half the fun. The sailors time their run so that a **whitewater** wave doesn't smash them back into shore. Once clear of the whitewater, the waves sloping into shore provide ramps for launching all kinds of aerials. The most spectacular are loops, and barrel rolls, in which the board, sail, and sailor all go end-over-end through 360 degrees.

With the power of a sail, windsurfers are able to do things on waves that ordinary surfers can only dream of. They speed around sections of whitewater, make powerful turns, and slide along the tops of waves.

Wave Sailing Part 2: Coming In

Riding a wave back in, the windsurfers pull off similar moves as surfers. They have the advantage of a sail to power them along, but the sail can get caught in the wave and cause a **wipeout**. Key wave riding moves include:

• Bottom turns: banking the board over at the base of the wave

• Off-the-lips: turning off the top of the wave and drops down the **face**

• Cutbacks: tightly turning to come back in the opposite direction

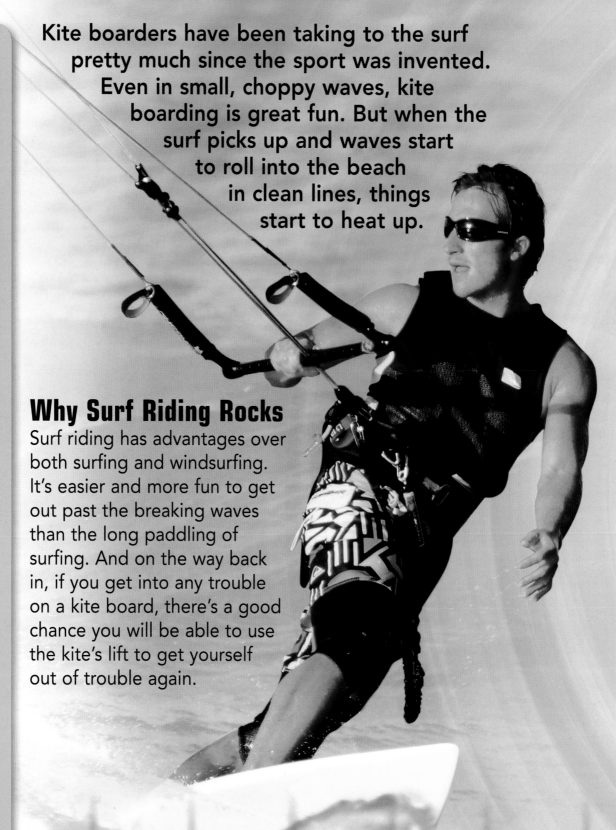

Kite boarders have been taking to the surf pretty much since the sport was invented. Even in small, choppy waves, kite boarding is great fun. But when the surf picks up and waves start to roll into the beach in clean lines, things start to heat up.

Why Surf Riding Rocks

Surf riding has advantages over both surfing and windsurfing. It's easier and more fun to get out past the breaking waves than the long paddling of surfing. And on the way back in, if you get into any trouble on a kite board, there's a good chance you will be able to use the kite's lift to get yourself out of trouble again.

Surf Riding Techniques

The techniques kite surfers use combine surfing, windsurfing, and skateboarding tricks, together with some moves you can only do on a kite board.

One move only kite surfers can do is called an aerial floater, which gets them over a section of whitewater. Using the power of the kite, they can cover much bigger distances than would be possible on a surfboard alone.

Even on a kite board, getting out through the breaking waves can be a challenge.

Top Two Surf Movies
- Big Windy—*filmed over an extended period in the Pacific islands, this movie combines an environmental message with some of the best wave riding ever seen.*
- Cape Reels—*shot in and around Cape Town, South Africa, this movie's highlight is probably the* offshore *big-wave action; there is plenty of smaller surf and freestyle fun, too.*

ON THE SCREEN

Surfers have ridden big waves for many years. But the biggest waves—over 50 feet (15 m) tall—are impossible for a surfer to catch in the usual way. So surfers developed the idea of tow-in surfing. Being towed up lets them catch bigger waves than ever before.

This rider is doing a beautiful off-the-lip **carve**. Timing is everything on a kite board. The kite must be pulling hard at just the right moment for a spectacular move like this one.

Tow-In Surfing Develops

In Hawaii in the 1990s, big-wave surfers such as Laird Hamilton began to spread the popularity of kite surfing. Some big-wave surfers used powerful kites to build up the speed needed to catch giant waves. However, they quickly moved on to using **personal watercraft (PWC)** to get towed into the surf. Surfers liked that they could drop the tow line once they caught the wave.

BIG-WAVE KITING

18

Big-Wave Kiting Today

Even though dedicated big-wave surfers no longer use kites, kite surfers still regularly tow themselves into the world's biggest surf. Kites are often spotted at famous big-wave spots such as Mavericks in California, Todos Santos in Mexico, Dungeons in South Africa, and Log Cabins in Hawaii.

Kite surfers can use waves as large, moving ramps. This kite surfer is performing a move called a lip bash, sending up a plume of water behind his board.

Laird Hamilton grew up in Hawaii, where he quickly became an excellent surfer. Today, Hamilton is known as one of the all-time great big-wave surfers, as well as one of the inventors of tow-in surfing. His most famous wave was one he rode at Teahupoo in Tahiti in 2000. The wave was so big, thick, and fast that it is often called "the heaviest wave ever ridden."

One of the fiercest rivalries between kite surfers and windsurfers is to see who can go fastest. For many years, windsurfers held the outright speed record for wind-powered watercraft. But when kite surfing hit the scene, things soon changed.

Windsurfers blasting back to the beach at Dahab, Egypt, where every year, you can see some of the fastest sailors in the world.

Kite Surfing Rules

In 2010, kite surfers grabbed the high-speed crown with a speed of 54.10 **knots** or 62.26 mph (100.19 kph). It was the first time any wind-powered craft had gone so fast. That same year, kite surfers broke the record twice more, ending with a record speed of 55.65 knots. In the meantime, windsurfing had fallen behind. The last time it held the speed record was in 2008, with a speed of 49.09 knots.

Lüderitz, Namibia

The battle for the speed record has been fought out largely at Lüderitz in Namibia. There, calm water and fiercely strong winds combine to create the best speed-sailing conditions on earth. Great white sharks lurk in the ocean off Lüderitz, but the racers don't have to worry about them—they're going too fast for a great white to catch them!

American kite surfer Rob Douglas sets a new world speed record at the 2010 Lüderitz Speed Challenge.

Speed Records Since 2008

Year:	Type of craft:	Place:	Speed (in knots):
2008	Windsurfer	Stes Maries de la Mer, France	49.09
2008	Kite surfer	Lüderitz, Namibia	49.84
2008	Kite surfer	Lüderitz, Namibia	50.26
2008	Kite surfer	Lüderitz, Namibia	50.57
2009	Hydrofoil trimaran	Hyeres, France	51.36
2010	Kite surfer	Lüderitz, Namibia	54.10
2010	Kite surfer	Lüderitz, Namibia	55.49
2010	Kite surfer	Lüderitz, Namibia	55.65

Most people enjoy going windsurfing or kite surfing for an hour or two. For some, however, this just isn't enough. They decide to race across large stretches of water or even spend weeks crossing huge oceans.

Long-Distance Ladies

Female kiters have made some of the most amazing long-distance kite crossings:

- Three-time world wave kiting champion Kirsty Jones set a new record in 2006, when she crossed the 140 miles (225 km) from the Canary Islands to Morocco in just 9 hours.

- In 2010, Natalie Clarke kited 150 miles (240 km) across Australia's Bass Strait in 9.5 hours.

- Also in 2010, Louise Tapper set a world record by kiting 1,245 miles (2,000 km) in 23 days.

Even kite surfing across a narrow channel, such as this one, for an hour or two is hard work. Imagine being a record-breaking long-distance kiter and traveling for hours on end!

Frenchman Arnauld de Rosnay was one of the first sailors to push the limits of how far a windsurfer could go. His adventures included:
- Sailing down the coast of the Sahara region
- Crossing the Bering Strait
- Making the voyage from Florida to Cuba

Sadly, de Rosnay disappeared in 1984 while trying to cross the Straits of Formosa between China and Taiwan.

Windsurfing Across Oceans

Windsurfers have used modified boards that allow the surfer to sleep in them, making for some huge long-distance trips:

- In 1997, American Steve Fisher windsurfed from California to Hawaii.

- In 2003, Frenchwoman Raphaela le Gouvello made a crossing from Peru to Tahiti. In 2006, she crossed the Indian Ocean.

Raphaela le Gouvello's board has sleeping quarters, storage space, and even a sink built into it.

There are all kinds of windsurfing and kite surfing competitions. They range from simple contests with friends to big world championships for **pros**.

Windsurfing Competition

Competitive windsurfers either have to be good at going fast or controlling the board.

- If they are good at going fast, either one-design racing (in which everyone uses the same design of board and sail) or slalom (racing around a course marked out with buoys) might appeal. One-design racing is a popular sailing event in the Olympics.

- Windsurfers who are good at board control can choose between wave riding and freestyle contests.

The giant sails used in one-design racing make the sailors look tiny.

Kite Surfing Contests

The most popular kite surfing contests are for wave riding and freestyle. These are the competitions that draw the biggest crowds, because they feature spectacular aerials, carves, and of course, high-speed crashes. There are also races around a pre-set course, hang time contests to see who can stay in the air longest, and competitions featuring kickers and sliders (ramps placed in the water).

Competitors on the beach wait for a kite surfing contest to begin.

The fresh air and exercise of windsurfing and kiting are good for you. But kiting and windsurfing can also be dangerous, so guidelines have been developed to help keep everyone safe.

Get Training

It's always important to get expert training when learning a new sport. This is especially true with activities such as windsurfing and kiting, which happen in a dangerous environment and with unfamiliar equipment to beginners. A qualified instructor makes sure that everyone learns in the safest way possible, without putting themselves or others in danger.

This kite surfer realized it's all gone wrong and "bailed"—let go of the kite's control bar and started to kick off his board.

Ride within Your Abilities

Windsurfing and kiting attract daredevil personalities. Surfers may be tempted to push themselves and go out in conditions that are harder than they are used to. This is never a good idea. They may be able to manage at first, but the wind or waves could pick up, drop, or change direction. Getting stranded and having to be rescued puts other people in danger as well.

Respect Other People

Share the water with everyone else: other kite surfers, windsurfers, sailors, canoeists, surfers, swimmers, paddlers—everyone. They all have a right to be there, so never get grumpy because it's too crowded. If you don't like the crowds, find a quieter place to surf.

Even the best windsurfers get it wrong sometimes. The important thing is to make sure no one else gets hurt by your mistakes!

Rules of the Road
- *When another sailor or kiter is coming towards you, always keep to your right.*
- *Never surf in a wind blowing straight offshore.*
- *When two kiters are sailing along (in the same or opposite directions), the upwind kite surfer should keep his or her **lines** high, to avoid getting tangled in the downwind kite's lines.*

Imagine you won the lottery and could book a ticket to go on a dream trip. Where would you go for some windsurfing or kite surfing kicks? There are hundreds of great places, but this list should give you a few ideas about where to start.

Tarifa, Spain

Probably the windsurfing and kite surfing capital of Europe, Tarifa sits on the southern coast of Spain, looking across the sea to Africa. Almost every afternoon the wind picks up, and spectators are treated to the sight of some of the world's best sailors and kiters practicing their moves.

Columbia River Gorge, Oregon

The Gorge is an unusual place for high-performance windsurfing and kite surfing because it is a river rather than an ocean or lake. There are wide stretches of water, spots with waves, high average wind speeds, and areas that are ideal for beginners.

Kite surfing in the cool, clear waters of Tarifa in Spain, which many say is the best place for wind and kite surfing in Europe

Ho'okipa, Hawaii

One guidebook says that "Ho'okipa is to windsurfers what Mount Everest is to mountaineers." This place on the island of Maui is one every wave sailor dreams of visiting. It's not for the faint-hearted, though—wipe out and there is a good chance you will be washed onto the rocks.

Diamond Head, Hawaii

Diamond Head is known as the best place for wave sailing on the island of Oahu. Any time the wind blows, there will be people rigging up brightly colored wave sails and carrying their boards down to the beach to test themselves in the surf.

Margaret River, Australia

One of Australia's most famous big-wave spots, Margaret River is not a place for beginner wind or kite surfers. The waves here can be huge, and the reefs make it a dangerous place to be washed ashore. It's a great place to watch the action, though, even if you don't go out.

Lake Arenal, Costa Rica

Created by a hydroelectric dam built in 1973, this giant lake took three years to fill up. Today, it is a high-wind destination for wind and kite surfers between November and April, and is excellent for freestyle and blasting.

Want to ride the biggest waves, surrounded by the world's best riders? Then head for the Hawaiian island of Maui.

blasting

windsurfing or kite surfing in a more-or-less straight line, going as fast as possible while throwing in turns, jumps, or other moves.

carve

a turn made with the board leaning over, throwing up a sheet of spray.

chop

little bumps on the surface of the water created by the wind blowing across it.

downwinder

kite surfing from one place to another that is farther downwind, which allows for traveling quickly and easily.

face

front part of a wave, before it has broken or fallen down on itself.

free riding

see *blasting*.

freestyle

a form of windsurfing or kite surfing that features jumps, slides, spins, and other tricks.

hang time

time spent in the air while doing a jump.

knots

units for measuring speed at sea or in the air; 1 knot = 1.15 mph (1.85 kph).

lines

strong cords connecting a kite surfer to the kite.

offshore

away from the shore; out to sea.

pros

professionals, people who are paid to do something as their job.

personal watercraft (PWC)

a powered water craft, similar to a water motorcycle; Jetski is a popular brand.

rigging up

putting a windsurfer together to go out sailing.

whitewater

the foamy water that appears when a wave breaks.

wipeout

a crash while surfing, windsurfing, or kite surfing.

Meditation Yoga

Oak Ridges Library

12:00 - 1:00 pm
Saturdays: April 29, May 27, June 10

De-stress and feel refreshed including tension-relieving stretches.

* As some people are chemically sensitive we respectfully request that you refrain from wearing any fragrances.

RICHMOND HILL PUBLIC

Library

Celebrate your curiosity

rhpl.richmondhill.on.ca

Drop-in!

No registration needed.

Organizations

The Pro Kiteboard Riders Association (PKRA) runs kite surfing competitions. There are competitions for wave riding, freestyle, and course racing. The contests are held all around the world at some of the best spots on earth for kiting. You can find out more at http://www.prokitetour.com.

The Professional Windsurfers Association (PWA) organizes some of the world's top-level professional windsurfing contests. As in kite surfing, there are contests for wave riding, freestyle, and course racing. Events take place all around the world, but most are held in Europe where windsurfing is especially popular. Find out more at http://www.pwaworldtour.com.

Websites

www.prokitetour.com/terminology-and-tricks-definition.php
Check out this site for kite surfing trick names and terminology.

www.windsurfing-academy.com/start_windsurfing/
why_windsurfing/beginner/windsurfing_glossary.asp
This site has a windsurfing glossary to help you talk like an expert.

http://www.raphaela-legouvello.com/index_an.php
Raphaela le Gouvella is one of the best long-distance windsurfers ever. Check out her technical guide to see her windsurfer board and the supplies she takes on her adventures.

INDEX